Caring

A Book About Caring

by Mary Small   illustrated by Stacey Previn

PICTURE WINDOW BOOKS
Minneapolis, Minnesota

Thanks to our advisors for their expertise, research, and advice:

Bambi L. Wagner, Director of Education
Institute for Character Development, Des Moines, Iowa
National Faculty Member/ Trainer,
Josephson Institute of Ethics - CHARACTER COUNTS!℠
Los Angeles, California

Susan Kesselring, M.A., Literacy Educator
Rosemount-Apple Valley-Egan (Minnesota) School District

Editorial Director: Carol Jones
Managing Editor: Catherine Neitge
Creative Director: Keith Griffin
Editor: Jacqueline A. Wolfe
Story Consultant: Terry Flaherty
Designer: Joe Anderson
Page Production: Picture Window Books
The illustrations in this book were created with acrylics.

Picture Window Books
5115 Excelsior Boulevard
Suite 232
Minneapolis, MN 55416
877-845-8392
www.picturewindowbooks.com

Printed in the United States of America.

Library of Congress Cataloging-in-Publication Data
Small, Mary.
Caring / by Mary Small ; illustrated by Stacey Previn.
p. cm. — (Way to be!)
Includes bibliographical references and index.
ISBN 1-4048-1049-8 (hardcover)
1. Caring—Juvenile literature. I. Previn, Stacey. II. Title. III. Series.
BJ1475.S62 2006
177.7—dc22   2005004277

When you care about people,

it matters to you what happens to them. You want them to be safe and happy. When they are sad or angry or frightened, you want to help.

You can care about your family, your friends, people who live in your neighborhood—even your pets.

There are lots of ways to show you care.

Bill offers to share his sucker with his older sister.

He is showing her he cares.

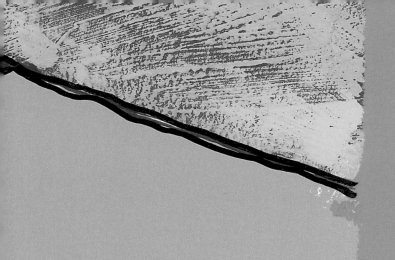

Even though sometimes it's hard,
Aaron keeps a close eye on his
brother and sister.

**He is showing them
he cares.**

On special days, Caroline makes sure everyone feels included.

She is showing she cares.

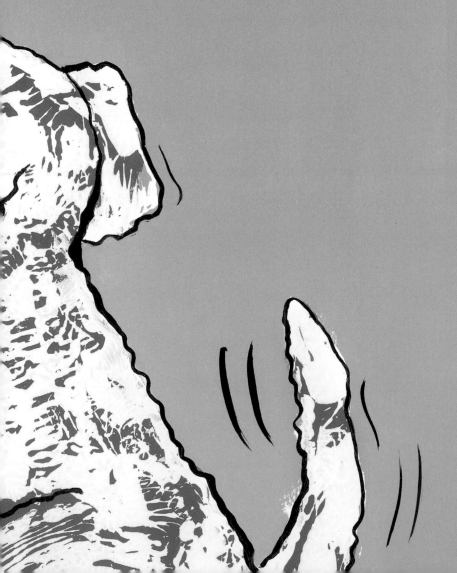

Joshua always holds the door open
to let other people go in first.

He is showing he cares.

Tim stops his friends from fighting and
helps them to make up.

He is showing he cares.

Nathan lets his best friend play with his favorite toy.

He is showing he cares.

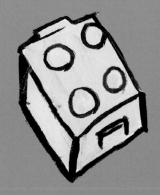

Freddie helps his dad work on the family car.

He is showing he cares.

17

Emily and Krista ask the new boy in school to sit with them during lunch.

They are showing they care.

Ashley goes out during a rainstorm
to help find her lost cat.

She is showing she cares.

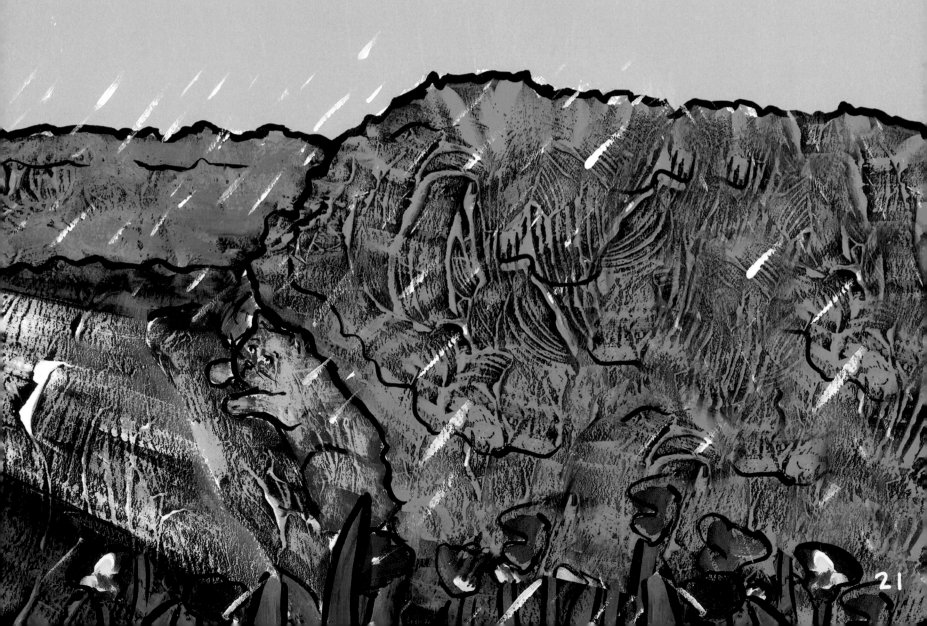

Mark and Alice share their favorite book.

They are showing each other they care.

At the Library

Bender, Marie. *Caring Counts*. Edina, Minn.: ABDO Publishing Co., 2003.

Nettleton, Pamela Hill. *May I Help You?: Kids Talk About Caring*. Minneapolis: Picture Window Books, 2005.

Raatma, Lucia. *Caring*. Mankato, Minn.: Bridgestone Books, 2000.

On the Web

FactHound offers a safe, fun way to find Web sites related to this book.

All of the sites on FactHound have been researched by our staff.

www.facthound.com

    1. Visit the FactHound home page.

    2. Enter a search word related to this book, or type in this special code: 1404810498

    3. Click the FETCH IT button.

Your trusty FactHound will fetch the best Web sites for you!

Index

Look for all of the books in the Way to Be! series:

Being Fair: A Book About Fairness

Being a Good Citizen: A Book About Citizenship

Being Respectful: A Book About Respectfulness

Being Responsible: A Book About Responsibility

Being Trustworthy: A Book About Trustworthiness

Caring: A Book About Caring